Presented to:

_____

Presented by:

_____

Date:

_____

THANKS
FOR BEING
A
MOM

Thanks for Being a Mom

©2004 ELM HILL BOOKS
ISBN: 1-40418-5305

The quoted ideas expressed in this book (but not scripture verses) are not, in all cases, exact quotations, as some have been edited for clarity and brevity. In all cases, the author has attempted to maintain the speaker's original intent. In some cases, quoted material for this book was obtained from secondary sources, primarily print media. While every effort was made to ensure the accuracy of these sources, the accuracy cannot be guaranteed. For additions, deletions, corrections or clarification in future editions, please contact Paul Shepherd, Executive director for Elm Hill Books. Email pshepherd@elmhillbooks.com

Manuscript written and compiled by Rebecca Currington
of Snapdragon Editorial Group, Inc.

Thanks for Being a Mom

Products from Elm Hill Books may be purchased in bulk for educational, business, fundraising, or sales promotional use. For information, please email SpecialMarkets@ThomasNelson.com

Additional copies of this book and other titles from
ELM HILL BOOKS are available from your local bookstore.

Other titles in this series:

Thanks for Being a Dad
Thanks for Being a Teacher
Thanks for Being a Friend

Introduction

Mothers may be young or old or somewhere in between. They may live nearby or far away or even in heaven. Regardless of their circumstances, they have partnered with God to give us life.

Thank You for Being a Mom is intended to celebrate all mothers—to serve as a reminder of the joy and sorrow, laughter and tears, toil and refreshing the office of motherhood affords. Let it move you to outwardly express your love and respect for those "mothers" who have graced your life.

So great was Jesus' thought for his own mother that he looked down from the cross, even as he was dying, and acknowledged her presence. Then he asked one of his disciples to treat her as his own.

Join with us as we honor and celebrate mothers everywhere!

The Publisher

*I*t's the three pairs of eyes that mothers

have to have ... one pair that sees through

closed doors ... another in the back of her head ...

and, of course, the ones in front that can look

at a child when he goofs up and reflect

"I understand and I love you" without

so much as uttering a word.

❋

ERMA BOMBECK

Table of Contents

oly as heaven a mother's tender love,

The love of many prayers and many tears

Which changes not with dim, declining years.

CAROLINE NORTON

A Mother's Love

Love never gives up, never loses faith, is always
hopeful, and endures through every circumstance.

1 CORINTHIANS 13:7 NLT

No language can express

the power and beauty and

heroism of a mother's love.

EDWIN H. CHAPIN

Love comes from God and those
who are loving and kind show that
they are the children of God, and that
they are getting to know him better.

1 JOHN 4:7 TLB

A mother's love is like God's love;

he loves us not because we are loveable,

but because it is his nature to love,

and because we are his children.

———— ✳ ————

EARL RINEY

This is the kind of love we are talking about—not that we once upon a time loved God, but that he loved us.

1 JOHN 4:10 MSG

*D*on't give up.

Just be patient and let God remind

you he's still in control.

———— ✳ ————

MAX LUCADO

A Mother's Faith

The only thing that counts is faith
expressing itself through love.

❋

GALATIANS 5:6 NIV

As a mother, my job is to take care of the possible and trust God with the impossible.

RUTH GRAHAM

Jesus said, "For mortals it is impossible,

but for God all things are possible."

MATTHEW 19:26 NRSV

*Y*our children learn more of
your faith during the bad times
than they do during the good times.

BEVERLY LAHAYE

Whenever you face trials of any kind,
consider it nothing but joy, because you
know that the testing of your faith
produces endurance; and let endurance
have its full effect, so that you may
be mature and complete,
lacking in nothing.

JAMES 1:2–4 NRSV

*E*very mother is like Moses,

she does not enter the promised land.

She prepares a world she will not see.

POPE PAUL VI

Faith is being sure of what
we hope for and certain of
what we do not see.

HEBREWS 11:1 NIV

Never despair of a child.

The one you were the most for

at the mercy seat may fill your

heart with the sweetest joys.

T. L. CUYLER

May those who sow in tears

reap with shouts of joy

--- ✳ ---

PSALM 126:5 NRSV

*I*f we want to keep our faith,

we must share it.

We must act.

——— ✳ ———

BILLY GRAHAM

A Mother's Instruction

Don't neglect your mother's teaching.
What you learn from them will crown you
with grace and clothe you with honor.

PROVERBS 1:8–9 NLT

25

The best academy,

a mother's knee.

JAMES RUSSELL LOWELL

All thy children shall be
taught of the LORD;
and great shall be the
peace of thy children.

ISAIAH 54:13 KJV

*S*tories first heard at a mother's knee

are never wholly forgotten—a little

spring that never quite dries up in

our journey through scorching years.

GIOVANNI RUFFINI

*She opens her mouth in skillful
and godly Wisdom, and on her
tongue is the law of kindness
[giving counsel and instruction].*

PROVERBS 31:26 AMP

hrough the ages no nation

has had a better friend than the

mother who taught her child to pray.

Devote yourselves to prayer;
keeping alert in it with an
attitude of thanksgiving.

COLOSSIANS 4:2 NASB

*P*arenthood is a partnership with God.

You are working with the Creator of the

universe in shaping human character

and determining destiny.

RUTH VAUGHN

We are labourers

together with God.

———— ✳ ————

1 CORINTHIANS 3:9 NIV

A Mother's patience is like

a tube of toothpaste—

it's never quite gone.

A Mother's Virtue

Clothe yourselves with compassion, kindness,
humility, gentleness and patience.
And over all these virtues put on love,
which binds them all together in perfect unity.

COLOSSIANS 4:12, 14 NIV

*K*ind words can be short

and easy to speak, but their

echoes are truly endless.

MOTHER TERESA

Let your conversation be always full of grace, seasoned with salt, so that you may know how to answer everyone.

COLOSSIANS 4:6 NIV

Mercy among the virtues is like

the moon among the stars.

It is the light that hovers

above the judgment seat.

EDWIN HUBBLE CHAPIN

Mercy triumphs over judgment.

JAMES 2:13 NASB

A mother is the person who

sits up with you when you are sick, and

puts up with you when you are well.

A Mother's Sacrifice

Hannah said, "I asked the Lord to give me this child,
and he has given me my request. Now I am giving him to
the Lord, and he will belong to the Lord his whole life."

1 SAMUEL 1:27–28 NLT

*T*hink of the sacrifice your mother

had to make in order that you might live.

Think of the sacrifice God had to make

that you and your mother might live.

This is love: not that we love God,
but that he loved us and sent his Son
as an atoning sacrifice for our sins.

1 JOHN 4:10 NIV

Mother means selfless devotion,

limitless sacrifice, and love

that passes understanding.

Since future victory is sure, be strong and steady, always abounding in the Lord's work for you know what nothing you do for the Lord is ever wasted.

1 CORINTHIANS 15:58 TLB

A man's work is from sun to sun,

but a mother's work is never done.

God helping you: Take your everyday,
ordinary life—your sleeping, eating,
going-to-work, and walking-around
life—and place it before God
as an offering.

———— ✳ ————

ROMANS 12:1 MSG

*N*othing else will ever make you

as happy or as sad, as proud

or as tired as motherhood.

ELIA PARSONS

A Mother's Joy

God has set you above your companions
by anointing you with the oil of joy.

———— ❋ ————

HEBREWS 1:9 NIV

*E*very mother has the breathtaking

privilege of sharing with God in the creation

of new life. She helps bring into existence

a soul that will endure for all eternity.

JAMES KELLER

O Lord, it was you who

formed my inward parts;

you knit me together in

my mother's womb.

PSALM 139:13 NRSV

*B*eautiful as seemed mama's face,

it became incomparably more lovely

when she smiled, and seemed

to enliven everything about her.

LEO TOLSTOY

The joy of the Lord is your strength.

NEHEMIAH 8:10 KJV

Mothers are like fine collectibles—

as the years go by they increase in value.

In Praise of Mothers

A good woman is hard to find, and worth far more than diamonds. Her children respect and bless her; her husband joins in with words of praise: "Many women have done wonderful things, but you've outclassed them all!"

※

PROVERBS 31:10, 27–29 MSG

MY MOM

Nice, beautiful
Pretty as a butterfly,
That's my mom.

Clever as a whale
Warm as a fuzzy bear.
That's my mom.

Soft as a pillow.
She laughs like an angel.
That's my mom.

Caring, cool, clever,
She's the best!
That's my mom!

JONATHAN, AGE 8

I love my mom because she let me get
a dog and then she let me sleep with it.
I hope she lives forever!

ANDEN, AGE 8

My mama is the best mama in the world.

She lets me share the chocolates

in her lamp table drawer.

She reads to me, and we sit

on the porch swing together.

BRENNA, AGE 6

I love my mom cause she lets
me read my book under the covers
with a flashlight and gives me
lots of chances to pick up my toys.

ETHAN, AGE 7

My mom is so cozy!

———✳———

EMILY, AGE 7

When God thought of mother,

he must have laughed with satisfaction

and framed it quickly—so rich, so deep,

so divine, so full of soul, power,

and beauty was the conception.

HENRY WARD BEECHER